Alimony, Child Custody, Divorce and Support in Pennsylvania

By

Crystal Tummala, Esq.

Attorney at Law

D1446862

Dedication

This book is dedicated to all of my precious children and to my remarkable husband Lok. This book is also dedicated to you, the reader.

TABLE OF TOPICS

Introduction

Throughout this book I have referred to the Pennsylvania Divorce Code. It is also known as The Domestic Relations Code.

The website for this resource can be found at:
http://www.legis.state.pa.us/WU01/LI/LI/CT/HTM/23/23.HTM

In addition, I have cited portions of The Pennsylvania Rules of Civil Procedure.

The website for this resource can be found at:
http://www.pacode.com/secure/data/231/partItoc.html

Bible references are from the New International Version.

This book is _not_ a substitute for legal advice.

Dear friend, if things feel as though they are going wrong in your life at this moment, pay attention to those feelings. This is not a book of judgment about who is right or wrong in your relationship or how you got to this point. The process of separation and divorce are a reality for almost 1 out of 2 marriages. The point is you have the right to make choices in your life.

I wrote this book to empower you and equip you with information so that you can move through this difficult process well informed.

I want you to be able to go after the best course of action for you. This course should be based on your individual needs and goals. These decisions will be suited to your circumstances. There is no such thing as a "cookie cutter" divorce, nor should there be. After all, this is your life we are talking about here!

It is my mission to see to it that as you set out reading this book, you will find it to be a practical resource guide.

This is a difficult time in your life. Besides perhaps a death, I cannot think of another time when you must make well thought out judgments while at the same time, you are feeling like your heart has been removed from your chest and that you cannot cry another tear. You need information so that you can make well-reasoned decisions.

I am a licensed attorney in the State of Pennsylvania. I am most familiar with the practices in western Pennsylvania. I will base my information and observations on the Pennsylvania Divorce Code and my knowledge and understanding specific to this state. This book is not intended to provide case specific legal advice.

As you go forward, continually keep in mind that your situation is unique to you. Divorce is a personal experience. This book is intended as an overview. Make sure you contact competent counsel who will review your situation and analyze your case. Don't make any decision unless you have peace in your heart about it.

Our Shared Vantage Point

I completely understand what you are going through. I have been through custody litigation and divorce myself. In fact, that event was the driving force of my decision to attend law school. While I was going through my divorce I felt helpless and unprepared for the entire experience.

I did not have a good resource book to reach for and I didn't know where to begin. I was too embarrassed to tell my friends about my fears and doubts. My parents and siblings never divorced so I didn't have family with experience to draw upon. I thought it would be too expensive for me to pay an attorney to sit there and explain everything to me and answer all of my questions. Besides, money was something I had very little of normally, and even less after my separation!

You may be feeling embarrassed that your marriage was not successful. You may sense that co-workers and family will judge you. You may feel that this is a personal failure and a poor reflection on you. I have heard many individuals share these same concerns.

This book can be a reference for you. It will help you understand this process, let you know what you can expect, and prepare you so that you do not lose your strength and focus.

Loss of Relationship

Even though we haven't met, I grieve for the loss of your relationship. I am sorry that, for whatever the reason, things did not work out for the two of you. The divorce process is emotionally draining. It is a disruption. I have heard it even called a "nightmare". It can seemingly take over your life, affect your health, and occupy your every waking thought.

Depending on whether you are the "Leavor" or the "Leavee" you are experiencing quite different emotions. If you are the Leavee, your identity has been attacked. How can this person reject you and your love and all that you have given to this relationship? Doesn't he/she appreciate all of the sacrifices you have made? What about everything you tolerated for the sake of the marriage? You were flexible!

What Happened?

Like most of us, you spent your childhood playing with dolls and a dollhouse or action figures. At times alone, and at other times with your friends. You were pretending about growing up and meeting your ideal husband or wife. Think back to how much of your teenage years were spent daydreaming and seeking that person you were meant to connect with.

One day it happened. Can you remember it? Your heart soared. You were special! You found that one person to give your love to and someone who loved you. No matter the size of the wedding, it was the most exhilarating day of your life. Then you started your day-to-day life together. At first, each day was filled with hope and fireworks. Happiness was yours. Maybe you bought a house. You settled in to your career. The children entered your lives and then one day, at one point, something changed. The feelings of love and anticipation were gone.

I had days where I felt like I was on an emotional roller coaster. I would feel mentally strong and think of all of the behaviors and character traits that I would no longer accept in future relationships and how I was going to improve myself. Then, I would talk to a friend who would ask how I was doing or I would suddenly remember a repair around the house that "he" used to do that now would fall on my shoulders. The anger would swell up in my stomach and then the sadness would overcome me.

Television was the worst. If I watched a movie that had a love scene, I wanted to throw something at the television. Sometimes, I would yell at the box about what a line of crap they were selling the public. "There is no LOVE. You can't trust anyone but yourself!" Can you tell that I was bitter?

"He gives strength to the weary and increases the power of the weak."-Isaiah 40:29

Guess what, all of these feelings are normal. I repeat, it is normal to feel anger. You may want revenge. You may want your former husband/wife to suffer. These feelings are to be expected. As you work through the process and time passes, the anger will decrease slowly but surely. Re-direct your energy and prepare to enter your future. I felt better after reading Psalm 143:7-8:

"Answer me quickly, Lord; my spirit fails. Do not hide your face from me or I will be like those who go down to the pit. Let the morning bring me word of your unfailing love, for I have put my trust in you. Show me the way I should go, for to you I entrust my life."

You need to let go of the emotional attachment to this marriage relationship. Focus on your future. Learn from yesterday. Experience is the source of wisdom. Use your wisdom and direct all of your energy toward this new season of your life. It will make you feel better if you make a list of your new dreams and goals.

Allow yourself to linger for a moment and picture the possibilities. Seasons change. Circumstances change. This exercise in future reflection will energize you. The excitement of possibility will motivate you.

When you are feeling like life is unstable, it may be helpful to list all of the other areas of life that have remained the same. You will come to see that your life still has a great foundation of stability.

What If I Don't Want It To Be Over And I Don't Want A Divorce?

If you have unresolved feelings then you should attempt to communicate your feelings to your spouse. Make an appointment with each other to sit down and talk. Have the conversation at the right time with the right words. Eliminate all distractions. Turn off the home phone ringer. Turn off the cell phones. Leave the television off. Don't have the computer in sight. Get a sitter for the kids. Set aside this time to speak from your heart. It is a starting point. The two of you can see if counseling is an option. Maybe you need more of these unplug and tune-in sessions with each other. Take what the two of you talk about from this session and do some self-analysis. Is there anything you can change? Is there anything you should change about yourself? Make sure that you take responsibility for whatever part of the problems you may be responsible for. Talk and see what expectations are missing or missed for each of you. If both are willing, then why can't it be saved?

If one spouse is set that the marriage is over and they are unwilling to put any work in to the relationship then, inevitably, it is sadly, over.

The Relationship Is Over, Now I Need A Lawyer

You have tried. You have had the talks. You have pled your case or listened to their case. The positions have not changed. You are heading down the road of divorce. Now you are in need of a lawyer.

A lawyer knows the law and the procedures to help you take the right steps. A lawyer and their client benefit by the lawyer being familiar with the assigned judge's individual preferences and personality. By knowing the judge, the facts of the case can be presented in the manner the judge will be more comfortable with.

How Do Attorneys Bill?

Attorneys generally set an initial retainer and then bill monthly as they do work. Once the retainer falls below a pre-set level, you will be asked to replenish the retainer.

Sources of Attorneys

Many people find an attorney from a recommendation from a friend, therapist, pastor, or their current attorney who doesn't work on family law matters. The internet can be a good source as you can search by geographic area. You can also refine your search to attorneys who handle family law issues. Another option is the bar association for your area. You can call them and request names of attorneys that practice in the area of Family Law.

Remember, as you interview attorneys by phone or in person, find out if they charge for the consultation. This question, asked up front, will eliminate surprises. A good attorney will give you their full attention during your meeting and show a genuine interest in you and your concerns. The attorney you eventually hire should work as a partner with you. The two of you will each do your share in the support and achievement of reaching your desired goals.

Your First Call To The Attorney

Attorneys have different approaches about how they handle first contacts with the office. Some attorneys have all initial calls go through their paralegal or legal secretary. The reasoning for this is that attorneys are in business just like everyone else. Often, if the caller knows they are speaking directly with an attorney, they will request legal advice from the attorney.

The other reason attorneys do not take the initial call is in case there is a conflict of interest. Conflicts can occur for a number of reasons but an obvious one is in case the other side has already had a consultation or hired this attorney to represent them.

Finally, another common reason that attorneys don't take intake calls is that they are busy drafting legal documents and appearing in court so they are unavailable to handle the new client intake telephone calls.

Whether the paralegal, secretary, or the attorney takes the initial call, you can expect to be asked the following:

First Phone Contact Information:

What is your name?

What is the best number for you to be reached at?

How long have you lived in Pennsylvania?

What is your spouse or significant other's name?

How did you hear about the firm?

What type of case is this: Custody, Divorce, Support?

Have you been served with any legal papers?

If so, when did you receive them?

What have you done with the papers so far?

Does the opposing party have an attorney?

If so, what is the name and phone number of their attorney?

What was your date of marriage?

What was your date of separation?

Do you have any children?

What are the names and ages of the children?

Who are the children living with now?

Where is everyone living at this time?

What county do you live in?

Is there any violence occurring in the home?

After going through these questions, the staff member should tell you the fee to meet with the attorney for a consultation. The consultation may be free, it may be a set fee, or it may be based on the attorney's hourly rate. If they don't tell you, or if you were unsure as to what they said, just ask.

If the attorney is the one screening the call then they may offer you a free phone consultation during that call. Some attorneys offer an initial in-person free consultation while others charge for it. Again, if unclear, just ask.

After this call think about how you feel. Did the attorney or his staff relax you and put you a bit at ease? Are the attorney's rates within your budget? Does this person sound like someone you could be comfortable with discussing very private matters?

Prior to your first meeting with the attorney you should start to get prepared. Preparation will save you time and money. It will give you something else to think about and you will feel good about putting order to your life and exercising control.

Collect the last 3 years of tax returns. See what current pay stubs you can locate and make a copy of these so you can document both you and your spouse's earnings. If practical, talk with your spouse and try to get an idea of all sources of income and what accounts you both have. Start to go through your family filing system and old mail. Get familiar with what you have and what you owe.

Do you feel your spouse may be hiding assets or spending? Do you want to locate possible hidden assets or spending that doesn't seem right? Follow your heart and investigate. Start by doing a line by line review of all of your credit card statements and bank statements. Are there charges on there that you don't recognize? Are there transfers to other accounts? Do you recognize those accounts? Are there withdrawals or deposits that seem excessive? You and your attorney can work together and also obtain the assistance of professionals such as an accountant if something looks out of place.

Locate the paperwork from the purchase of the home. Copy the papers you received the day you bought the house. Particularly, the ones showing the purchase price and obtain a copy of the sales agreement. Get a copy of the deed if you have it. You may also be able to go on the county website and get a copy of the deed so you can see exactly how the names are listed on the deed.

Find the most recent statement for the cars. Try to locate the paperwork from the purchase of the cars and make a copy.

Locate all statements for bank accounts and make copies of the statements. Next is the Retirement Accounts. Locate information and statements on you and your spouse's pensions and retirement accounts whether it is called a 401(k), 403(b), 457(b) or thrift savings account. Any statements or balances on those should be located and copied. Think about any assets accumulated during your marriage as well as the increases in value of anything owned before the marriage.

What about debts? Any debts incurred during the marriage by either party are most likely marital debts and will also need to be divided up.

Is there a business? If so, that will need to be valued by a professional but start to collect any records you have access to and start to make copies for your records.

Do you have life insurance policies? I am not talking about term life policies but others kinds such as whole life-cash value policies. Locate and copy those policies. See if you can find any records of loans taken out against these as well.

What about your jewelry? Do you have jewelry? How about collectibles, artwork, and furniture? Have you itemized and made copies of the records and inventoried the safe deposit box?

Did you and your spouse sign a Prenuptial Agreement? If so, locate it, read it, and give a copy of it to your attorney so that he/she can begin their review and analysis of it.

You will need to open your own account to get your own financial life established. Be bold and get things started.

You may be asked by your attorney to keep a diary so that when you speak to them, you can talk about what you have recorded and observed since you last spoke. For instance, if your spouse returned the children 25 minutes late and it is becoming a pattern that may be something to note in your journal for your next conversation with your attorney.

How Do I Tell My Partner/Spouse That It Is Over?

I put this here because sometimes people do pre-planning prior to telling their spouse that it is over. You may want to speak with an attorney to go over what you can expect and how you will be financially impacted by a divorce. You may want to get some advice about amounts you can expect to receive/pay for child support or alimony/spousal support. You may just be procrastinating over having the dreaded discussion. There are numerous reasons.

Now let's suppose you are the one breaking the news. How do you do it? Is it better to do it in public or in private? Think of the other person's personality. This might be a good place for a reminder of the Golden Rule to "do unto others as you would have others do unto you." So, how would you want to be told? Think through the conversation. How do you think, based on everything you have come to know about him/her, what their reaction will be?

There is no correct answer as to whether to tell them it is over in public versus in private. Whether it is done in private or in public it will be a painful conversation. If there is a history of abuse and you are in fear of a violent reaction, you are able to file for a Protection from Abuse Order. Each county has its own process. Discuss these concerns and the process with your lawyer. If you do not have a lawyer, then contact your county court or legal aid office. There are volunteers who can even provide forms and provide procedural information on how to complete them.

If you were the one on the receiving end of the conversation ending the relationship, please take comfort in this:

"The LORD is with me; I will not be afraid."-Psalm 118:6

"In God, whose word I praise— in God I trust and am not afraid. What can mere mortals do to me?"-Psalm 56:4

What About Telling Our Children?

It is a hard thing to decide when and how to tell the children. For the two of you, maybe it is best to discuss how you both want that conversation to take place. Once you have agreed on the time and place to talk with the children, maybe the two of you should talk with the children together. This is a good thing to do because this will be the first of many conversations the two of you will have about how to handle situations involving the children.

The children are going to have questions. It should be made clear to the children that they are, in no way, to blame for the breakup of the marriage. They need to know that you will always be their mom/dad and that both of you will always love them. The children will want to know where mom and dad will be living and where they will be living. Make sure they know when they will get to see the parent they are not going to be living with.

No matter how draining and overwhelming all of this is, you have to keep the children your focus. This is the time to continue your involvement in their lives. If you have not been at your best, re-concentrate your efforts. This is the time to get informed about the children. Even if there is friction about the custody of the children, don't keep the other spouse from seeing the children unless there is violence and you have pursued your legal remedies. Never, ever, ever use the children as a sword to achieve revenge against the spouse because it will be the children who are harmed.

Time To Take An Inventory

If your divorce complaint includes a request for equitable distribution, Pennsylvania Rule of Civil Procedure 1920.33, will require you (or your attorney) to file an inventory within 90 days of the filing of the complaint.

Inventory Worksheet

Assets of the Parties

Real Property

What is the value of the property?

When was it purchased?

What was the purchase price of the house?

How much is owed on the mortgage or mortgages?

What is the monthly payment amount?

Who lives in the house?

How do you want to handle the house (do you want to keep it or dispose of it)?

Do you own other real estate?

Is there real estate that is not marital property?

If so, please explain.

Please tell me about your cars:

Make   Model   Year   Vin#
Current Value

Make   Model   Year   Vin#
Current Value

Checking Account/s
Name   Account number balance

Savings Account/s
Name   Account number balance

IRA
Name   Account number balance

Do you or your spouse have a
pension/profit sharing plan?
Name account value

List all retirement accounts
Name account value

Bonds or certificates of deposit
Name Account # Value

Do you have a safe deposit box and what does it contain?

What is the value of each item in the box?

Trusts Name   value

Life Insurance policies (with a cash value) What is the face value and cash surrender value?

Have either of you received an inheritance? If so, who was it to and who was it from? What was the amount?

Do you have any annuities?

Do you have any patents, copyrights, inventions, or receive any royalties, if so, explain.

Do you or your spouse own a business?

What are your other marital assets?

Liabilities

Please list all debts including credit
cards.

Creditor Name   Name on Debt
Balance (as of date of Separation)

Continue this list for each creditor.

    Debts will be divided just like the
assets. If all of the debts are not
known, a good source to review is your
credit report. All debt information
should be pursued as part of the
discovery process.

What About Bankruptcy?

Sometimes, when the amount of debt that has been accumulated and the inability to pay becomes clear, it may make sense for you to jointly file for bankruptcy before divorcing. If you file together you can have one filing fee and one bankruptcy attorney. As long as you are married, even if living apart, you can file jointly.

We Have Divided Everything
Up Ourselves, Do I Still
Need An Attorney?

Even if things have worked out amicably up to this point and you think you have divided up everything, you still need to see your own lawyer. Your lawyer can review any agreement or terms you and your partner have come up with. Your lawyer can give you an overview of the process and inform you of your rights. Either you will find out that you covered everything or you may find out there were items or terms that were missed. You may find out that you have rights that you didn't even know about.

Get your attorney's advice before you sign any agreement.

Your First Meeting With An Attorney

When you have a first meeting with
an attorney you should expect to complete
an information sheet.

The attorney, or his staff member,
may send you out the form in advance and
ask you to bring it with you to the
appointment. If not, it is a matter of
attorney preference if the forms are
given to you to complete in the waiting
room or if the attorney will complete
these items line by line during the first
part of the appointment.

These are the types of information
you can expect to provide:

CLIENT INFORMATION FORM

Date: _____

Full Name: _____

Maiden Name: _____

Do you plan on resuming this name after
the divorce? ___

Address (this is where letters from me
will come to): _____

_____

City: _____

State: ___

Zip code: _____

County: _____

How long have you lived at your present
address? ____

How long have you lived in Pennsylvania?_____

Do you own or rent your home? _____

Do you live in an apartment, a house or other
living arrangement, please
describe:_____

_____

How many bedrooms are in the home? _____

Do you, or have you ever, had any criminal
charges filed against you?____

If yes, explain _____

Do you have any substance abuse issues or
mental health issues? _____

If yes, please explain: _____

_____

Do you and your spouse have a Prenuptial
Agreement? _____

If so, please give details and provide a copy
to me as soon as possible

Is your spouse in the military?

If yes, where? _____

Mailing Address: (if different from you
regular address)

_____

_____

_____City: _____

State: __   Zip code:_____

Prior address: _____

_____

City: _____

State: ___   Zip code:_____

Home Phone #   _____

Work Phone #   _____

Cell Phone #   _____

Email address: _____

Your date of birth: _____

Social Security Number: _____

Driver's License Number: _____

What is your place of

employment?_____

_____

How long have you been with this

employer?   _____

What is your work schedule?

_____

_____

What is the school district where you reside?

_____

Educational Background

What is your highest level of education?

_____

Do you have any degrees?_____

If so, from where and what was the date you earned the degree? _____

_____

Do you have any professional licenses? _____

Do you hold any certifications? _____

Date of Marriage: _____

Date of Separation: _____

City and State of the Marriage:

_____

Are you currently involved in any lawsuits?

_____

If so, what was the date of injury or of the incident _____

What is the case number and where is the case filed at? _____

What is the current status of the case?

_____

_____

_____

Current Gross Income (per year):

$_____

Do you have any current health problems?

_____

_____

Do you have any prior health problems?

_____

If yes, explain

_____

_____

Do you have any disabilities? ____

If yes, explain

_____

_____

Spouse/Ex-Spouse/Partner's Name:

_____

Address: _____

_____

City: _____ State: _____

Zip Code: _____

County: _____

How long has the other parent lived at

this address?: _____

What is their highest level of education?

_____

Do they have any Degrees? _____

If so, please provide date obtained and from where: _____

_____

Do they hold any Professional Licenses?

_____

Do they have any Trade certifications?

_____

Do they gave any current health problems?

_____

_____

_____

Do they have any prior health problems?

_____

_____

Are they currently involved in any lawsuits?

____

If so, what was the date of injury or of the incident? _____

_____

_____

What is the case number and where is the case filed at? _____

_____

Do they own or rent? ____

What is their living arrangement i.e.,
apartment, house or other arrangement?

_____

_____

How many bedrooms do they have? ____

Who lives with them?

_____

_____

_____

Home # _____

Cell # _____   Work # _____

Who is their employer? _____

_____

What is their work schedule?

_____

What is their work history?_____

_____

What school district do they live in?

_____

Does the other party have any criminal
charges? ___

If yes, please explain:

Does the other party have any substance abuse issues? ___

If yes, please explain:

_____

_____

Does the other party have any mental health issues? _____

Does the other party have an attorney? ___

If so, what is their name?

_____

Attorney Address: _____

City: _____ State: ___ Zip:_____

Attorney Phone Number: _____

Attorney Fax Number: _____

Attorney Email Address: _____

Spouse/ Ex- Spouse / former Partner's Social Security Number: _____

Date of Birth: _____

Spouse/Partner Gross Income per year:

_____

Maiden Name: _____

Has either spouse been previously married? ___

Have you been married before? ___

If so, to who: _____

What was the Date of Divorce:

_____

What was the location of the Divorce?:

_____

Are their Children? _____

Name: _____

Date of Birth: _____ Age: _____

Name: _____

Date of Birth:_____ Age: _____

Name: _____

Date of Birth: _____ Age:_____

Name: _____

Date of Birth: _____ Age: _____

Name: _____

Date of Birth:_____ Age: _____

Name: _____

Date of Birth: _____ Age:_____

Where are the children living?

_____

_____

Please provide all addresses the children
have lived at for the last 5 years.

_____

_____

What schools/childcare centers do the children attend? _____

Please list any extracurricular activities the children are involved in? _____

What is the distance between your home and the other parent's home? _____

Do the children attend church or other religious services? _____

If yes, please provide the name of the church and when they attend:_____

Are there children (not of this marriage/relationship)? _____

Name: _____
Date of Birth: _____   Age:_____
School: _____
Name: _____
Date of Birth: _____   Age:_____
School: _____

Name: _____

Date of Birth: _____   Age:_____

School: _____

Current custody arrangement:

_____

Has custody ever been determined by a court? ____

If so, what was the date of the order:
Provide a copy of the Order.

Are there any people with significant involvement in the child's life such as family, friends, or teachers? _____

What is your ideal custody schedule? __

Your attorney will need documents to begin to work on your case. You should be prepared for your first meeting if you provide:

- You and your spouse's latest three (3) pay stubs
- Your most recent tax return

- A copy of appraisals for any real estate you own
- A copy of all real estate deeds
- A copy of you and your spouse's most recent statements for all 401(k), investments and retirement plans.

Whether or not you hire the attorney, what you chat about in this first meeting is privileged. This means that the attorney cannot be forced to disclose what either of you discussed during that meeting. In order to assure that what you relay is privileged, do not take other people in to the meeting with you. If you decide to bring someone with you for moral support and comfort, have them wait for you in the reception area.

When you look for an attorney, make sure they are committed to your case. They should be dependable. Plan your calls and visits with your attorney so that they will be effective and productive.

Be an active listener when your attorney speaks to you. If you are given homework, it is to your benefit to complete it.

It will save you time and money. Give thought to who you hire as your legal counsel. This is a trying path you are going down and who you choose to walk with on this path is a critical decision.

Should I Move Out Of The Apartment/House?

When you are trying to decide whether to remain in the marital home or move out, seek advice from your attorney. There may be reasons that you should remain in the house in order to fully protect your legal rights. If you have children, do they really need more change right now? Would it be best for them?

Before anyone makes a decision to move, it is best to go around the house from room-to-room and inventory each room. Take pictures or video as well. Start to collect all of your financial records. Obtain paperwork for major assets such as: receipts, deeds, brokerage statements, etc. These things may intentionally or unintentionally become unavailable once a move is made.

If the best decision for your situation is to move out, then you must look at your income and expenses to see what you can afford-at least temporarily. If you are fortunate enough to have close family or friends who have extra space, that may be the best option in terms of costs and invaluable moral support.

If there is an emergency situation contact: local housing assistance agencies, churches, or shelters for housing options. Discuss your wishes and your concerns with your attorney as courts have power, depending on the facts/circumstances of the case, to grant exclusive possession of the marital home.

If you do move out, then make sure that you notify the postal service and anyone else necessary of your new address so that your personal mail does not continue to go to the prior address. Make sure you notify your attorney of your new address right away so that you receive these confidential letters personally.

Change and Loneliness

Whether you physically move out of the marital residence or not, there will be times when you will feel lonely. This will give you a chance to get to know yourself again. You will motivate yourself and you will be encouraged as your thoughts become clear. Clarity is power.

It is written in Psalm 25:16-17, "Turn to me and be gracious to me, for I am lonely and afflicted. Relieve the troubles of my heart and free me from my anguish."

What extraordinary gifts and talents do your children have that you can nurture even more with this change in your life? Have a goal. Create a photograph in your mind of the future you want to create. Understand timing. Goals change. You dreams change. You will have transitions in your life. Be good to yourself. Carefully document what's happening in your life. You can later look back and reflect on this time.

The Internet And Social Media

Be careful about the statements you make on the internet and the pictures that you post. Also keep track of what your spouse is posting. If you do not have direct access to their postings, perhaps you have a friend in common that can keep a look-out for anything you should be aware of.

People are more relaxed and let their guard down when they post on the internet. Pictures showing or suggesting drug use or adultery can be damaging to a divorce or custody case.

This should also get you thinking. If you have friends in common and you don't want your former partner to have access to information about your social life, directly or indirectly, it may be best to unfriend those mutual friends for the time being. Think before you post in general.

If you believe that there are emails showing an inappropriate relationship between your spouse and another, then make your attorney aware of it so that they can try to obtain these emails through the discovery process.

Can I Get <u>Legally</u> Separated In Pennsylvania?

In Pennsylvania, there is not a court-issued document that states the parties are legally separated.

Instead, separation is based on intention. It has to be the intention of the parties to live separate and apart. The ways to demonstrate living separate and apart include: no longer sharing the same bedroom, having separate banking accounts, no longer attending social events together, no longer sharing meals together, and/or living apart. If a separation date is not established, it shall be assumed to be the date the divorce complaint was served.

Once the parties are separated, the financially dependent party can apply for spousal support. This is something to discuss with your attorney as your partner may object to spousal support depending on your specific facts and situation.

Separation Agreement

It is possible to have a Separation Agreement. Both parties must sign a Separation Agreement for it to be valid.

This agreement would cover how the property and debt is to be split up and it can outline an agreed amount for spousal and/or child support.

This agreement can only come about if both parties agree. Be sure that any agreement is what you want before you sign it. Why, because later on it can be brought to court to show what was already agreed to if you would later change your mind and want something different.

If possible, I think it would be sensible to have the agreement drafted, or at a minimum reviewed, by your legal counsel prior to signing it.

Domestic Violence

If you are faced with issues of abuse or domestic violence, I urge you to protect yourself. Protection is available in Pennsylvania through a Protection from Abuse Order.

Within Section 6102 of the Code, Abuse is defined as: the occurrence of one or more of the following acts between family or household members, sexual or intimate partners or persons who share biological parenthood:

(1) Attempting to cause or intentionally, knowingly or recklessly causing bodily injury, serious bodily injury, rape, involuntary deviate sexual intercourse, sexual assault, statutory sexual assault, aggravated indecent assault, indecent assault or incest with or without a deadly weapon.

(2) Placing another in reasonable fear of imminent serious bodily injury

(3) The infliction of false imprisonment

(4) Physically or sexually abusing minor children

(5)   Knowingly engaging in a course of conduct or repeatedly committing acts toward another person, including following the person, without proper authority, under circumstances which place the person in reasonable fear of bodily injury.

For further review please see 23 PaC.S.A. Section 6102.

Divorce

How Can I Get A Divorce

In Pennsylvania?

The quick overview is that Pennsylvania has both fault and no fault divorce. Almost all divorces are now completed as no fault divorces. They can be completed fairly quickly as long as there are no complex economic factors. When there is mutual consent that the marriage is irretrievably broken, 90 days have passed since the divorce was filed, and both parties consent and file affidavits-the Court can then grant a divorce.

If there is not a mutual agreement the parties will have to live separate and apart for 2 years before one can proceed with a unilateral divorce.

The biggest delay in divorces, beyond the minimum waiting periods for a mutual or unilateral divorce, is unresolved economic issues. It is important that all economic issues are dealt with prior to the divorce being granted. If you wait until the divorce is finalized you could lose significant financial rights. These issues include: equitable distribution of property, alimony, alimony pendente-lite, spousal support, counsel fees, court costs, and expenses.

Now to explain a little deeper, in Pennsylvania, under the Divorce Code, there are 3 ways to obtain a divorce as long as one of the parties has been a Pennsylvania resident for at least 6 months immediately prior to filing the divorce complaint. The first way is by consent of both parties. The divorce is filed and served on the other party. There is a 90 day waiting period. After the 90 days, if no other issues have been raised or if all issues are resolved, then the request for the entry of the divorce decree can be made to the court.

The second way to obtain a divorce is by living separate and apart for 2 years. After the 2 years, either party can request the entry of a divorce decree, provided the divorce complaint was filed and served on the other party. Again, prior to requesting entry of a divorce decree under this section of the Pennsylvania Divorce Code, make sure all economic claims have been settled by Court Order or by agreement prior to entry of the divorce decree

The third way to obtain a divorce is based on fault. This would be filed by, and found in favor of, an "innocent and injured" spouse. There are specific grounds for divorce under this section of the Code. Grounds include desertion; committed adultery; endangered the life or health of the other spouse; been sentenced to prison for two years or more, or offered indignities to the innocent spouse to make their life intolerable and burdensome.

Because of the availability of the other methods of obtaining a divorce, this method is not used with any regularity. How many people are completely innocent victims and want to air all of their private life to the court?

As with the other ways of obtaining a divorce, I repeat, it is important that all economic issues have either been settled by order of court or by agreement by the parties prior to the entry of the divorce decree.

What If I Signed, Or They Signed, A Prenuptial Agreement?

If there is a prenuptial agreement, it is up to the party that wants to challenge it to provide clear and convincing evidence that it should be set aside.

In Pennsylvania, the agreement can be set aside if it is proven that the party did not execute the agreement voluntarily or if the party wasn't provided reasonable disclosure of the property and financial obligations of the other party. Also, the agreement cannot cover child support or child custody. The party making the challenge would have to show that they didn't provide a written waiver of the required disclosure and that they did not have adequate knowledge of the property and finances or financial obligations before signing the agreement.

It is a high burden of proof to meet and the court will not look at the fairness of the agreement.

What Happens If I Need The Judge To Decide Something On My Case?

Do I Have To Wait For A Trial?

Motions Court

Motions Court is a different type of court proceeding. In Motions Court temporary or more immediate matters are heard. Examples include: temporary custody or a change to a visitation schedule to attend a wedding.

The lawyer will draft the specific facts of what you are seeking. You will sign a verification that the facts are correct. If appropriate, they will attach exhibits such as email, a bank statement, etc. The attorney will get a copy to the judge, sign up for the motion to be put on the calendar to be heard, and supply the other side's attorney with a copy of the motion for their review.

After receipt of the motion, the other attorney will review and discuss it. They may have evidence or a position in opposition. They will be opposing the motion. Their response will also be provided to your attorney and to the judge depending on the judge's preferences.

The day of Motion's Court arrives. The attorneys make oral arguments before the judge so that he/she can make a ruling on the motion.

Discovery

Part of your case will involve formal or informal discovery. Discovery can include: depositions, interrogatories, and production of documents.

Discovery is a valuable process to gather information. The type of items that are typically requested are: bank statements, credit card statements, investment account statements, 401(k)/other retirement accounts as well as pension information, deeds, and insurance policies.

Discovery can include depositions. This is answering questions under oath. Your/their answers will be taken down by a stenographer and provided back to the attorneys in the form of a transcript. This transcript is then reviewed by the spouses and their attorneys.

You or the other party can also be served with a list of written questions known as interrogatories.

If the marital estate includes a business then you will probably want to hire a business valuation expert. Discuss this with your attorney. Businesses are usually valued using one of three approaches.

The first approach is the Income Approach. This valuation examines the business based on cash flow. The second valuation method is the Asset Centered Approach. This approach calculates the value of the business based on the value of inventory. The third approach is Market Approach. This value analyzes the values of comparable businesses.

Custody

One of the most emotional issues in divorce is the custody of the children. These are definitions and types of custody as they are defined by the Divorce Code:

Legal Custody can be either shared or sole.

Shared Legal Custody gives the right to legal custody to more than one person.

Sole Legal Custody gives legal custody to one person.

There are various types of Physical Custody.

The first type is Shared Physical Custody.

Shared physical custody can be the ideal arrangement under the right circumstances.   Each individual would have significant time with the child. For this arrangement to be successful the parents should live near each other. Also, this form of custody relies on two parents who are able to effectively communicate with each other for its success.

The next type is <u>Primary Physical Custody</u>. With Primary Physical Custody, one individual has custody most of the time. <u>Partial Physical Custody</u> is when one individual has physical custody of the child less than the majority of the time. When there is <u>Sole Physical Custody,</u> that individual has exclusive physical custody of the child.

In some situations, such as abuse, there is also <u>Supervised Physical Custody</u>. In this situation, the time together between the party and the child is monitored by a designated adult or through an agency that has agreed to provide supervision services.

Regardless of how the custody arrangement is labeled, all children need love. They need to feel secure now more than ever. Isn't this a need we all share?

Even if the two of you are no longer going to be married or in a relationship with each other, you are still partners in parenting. You still need to parent the children together. You will need to have a regular method of communication. Both parents need to keep each other informed about what is going on with the children's schooling.

Are there any upcoming medical or dental appointments? How will decisions about your children be made? Will one parent make all of the major decisions? Will you have meetings or telephone calls to discuss upcoming decisions?

If custody is going to be an issue in your case then it is a good idea to list and identify who is currently attending to the various needs of the child/children.

Use this list in the way that works best for you. You can either make check marks in the column or just mentally take an inventory of a sampling of the needs of a child.

Parenting Inventory

<u>You</u>   <u>other parent</u>

Taking them to and from
Daycare

Taking them to and from
dentist appointments

Taking them to and from
doctor appointments

Shopping for their clothes
and hygiene products

Shopping for their food?

Who handles their discipline?

Who attends open houses
and teacher conferences?

Who takes them to and from
their extracurricular activities?

Who maintains the children's
hair, nails, and teeth?

Who helps with their homework?

Who packs their lunch?

Who does the children's
laundry?

Who prepares the children's
meals?

Who watches them when they
aren't in daycare or
at school?

Who bathes the children and
washes their hair?

Who Can File For Custody Of A Child?

Section 5324 of the Divorce Code lists who has standing to file for any form of physical custody or legal custody. Parents can always file for custody. A person who stands "in loco parentis" (in the place of a parent) can have standing as well.

When one party files a complaint for custody, the parties often have to attend some form of an education seminar. In most cases children are also required to attend the kid's version of the seminar as well. The class is intended to explain an outline of the custody process and how important and useful it is for the two of you to be able to communicate with each other. When the class is over a Certificate of Completion is issued. Some counties want this Certificate of Completion filed with the court.

Mediation And Conciliation

The next phases to attempt to resolve the custody dispute are Mediation and Conciliation. These processes are intended to try again at getting the parties to see what they can agree on and narrow down what they don't agree on. The hope is that an agreement can be reached rather than having to continue to litigate.

Since the person in mediation with you is the co-participant in endless past arguments, try to listen like you are hearing what they have to say for the very first time. You will have a fresh perspective. The court has made provisions for cases involving issues of domestic violence. Discuss this with your lawyer if it applies to your case.

Mediation is constructive in certain situations. It works for couples who are communicating on a civil level. These couples are somewhat willing to negotiate in order to move on with the rest of their lives. They are willing to demonstrate flexibility on some things in the hope of reducing the time and expense of continued litigation.

If you are in mediation and things get too "emotionally heated" take a break. Once emotions have calmed you can then re-group and continue. After negotiations, mediation and conciliation, if an agreement is not reached-then the case will move on to a hearing and/or trial.

Psychological Evaluations

Psychological evaluations may be ordered by a judge, a hearing officer or a custody officer. These are usually ordered in shared, primary, and sole custody cases. These evaluations are expensive. The costs are allocated between both parties.

The evaluation process involves the parties completing questionnaires. The parties undergo psychological tests. The parties and the children are interviewed over the course of several meetings. The parents are also observed in at least one session each with their children to see how they relate to each other. The evaluator will often interview other parties such as grandparents, new spouses or significant others.

Once the evaluations are complete a report is issued to the parties and their counsel. The report will be used to aid in settlement. It will be a point of strength to the party it favored as courts tend to give significant weight to the custody recommendation.

Parenting Plan

What is in a parenting plan? In custody cases where an agreement is not being reached by the parties, the court may require the parties, under Section 5331 of the Divorce Code, to submit a parenting plan. The plan acts as an aid to the court in the disputed custody case. This plan will cover the care and custody of the child.

A parenting plan should cover the schedule for personal care and control of the child, including parenting time, holidays and vacations. It should encompass the education and religious involvement, if any, of the child. It should cover the health care of the child. It covers transportation arrangements. The agreement should also address what happens when someone breaches the custody order or if there is a dispute or a desire to make changes to it.

Guardian Ad Litem

Based on the level of conflict in the case and the complexity of the issues, the court may appoint, under Section 5334, a Guardian ad litem for the children. The Guardian will represent the child in the action. The court may assess the cost upon the parties or any of them or as otherwise provided by law. The guardian ad litem must be an attorney at law.

(b) Powers and duties.--The guardian ad litem shall be charged with representation of the legal interests and the best interests of the child during the proceedings and shall do all of the following:

(1) If appropriate to the child's age and maturity, meet with the child as soon as possible following the appointment and on a regular basis thereafter.

(2) On a timely basis, be given access to relevant court records, reports of examination of the parents or other custodian of the child and medical, psychological and school records.

(3) Participate in all proceedings.

(4) Conduct such further investigation necessary to ascertain relevant facts for presentation to the court.

(5) Interview potential witnesses, including the child's parents and caretakers, if any. The guardian ad litem may examine and cross-examine witnesses and present witnesses and evidence necessary to protect the best interests of the child.

(6) Make specific recommendations in a written report (to the court relating to the best interests of the child, including any services necessary to address the child's needs and safety. The court shall make the written report part of the record so that it may be reviewed by the parties. The parties may file with the court written comments regarding the contents of the report. The comments filed by the parties shall also become part of the record.

(7) Explain the proceedings to the child to the extent appropriate given the child's age, mental condition and emotional condition.

(8) Advise the court of the child's
wishes to the extent that they can be
ascertained and present to the court
whatever evidence exists to support the
child's wishes. When appropriate because of
the age or mental and emotional condition
of the child, determine to the fullest
extent possible the wishes of the child and
communicate this information to the court.
A difference between the child's wishes
under this paragraph and the
recommendations under paragraph (6) shall
not be considered a conflict of interest
for the guardian ad litem.

(c) Abuse.--If substantial allegations
of abuse of the child are made, the court
shall appoint a guardian ad litem for the
child if:

(1) counsel for the child is not
appointed under section 5335 (relating to
counsel for child); or

(2) the court is satisfied that the
relevant information will be presented to
the court only with such appointment.

(d) Evidence subject to examination.--A guardian ad litem may not testify except as authorized by Rule 3.7 of the Rules of Professional Conduct, but may make legal argument based on relevant evidence that shall be subject to examination by the parties.

So if my partner and I can't agree, how will the judge decide the custody arrangement for us?

The Sixteen Custody Factors

The New 16 Factors Used to Determine Custody

In Pennsylvania, there are sixteen factors, under Section 5328 of the Code, that are to be used by judges to decide issues of child custody. These are the factors:

(a) Factors.--In ordering any form of custody, the court shall determine the best interest of the child by considering all relevant factors, giving weighted consideration to those factors which affect the safety of the child, including the following:

(1) Which party is more likely to encourage and permit frequent and continuing contact between the child and another party.

(2) The present and past abuse committed by a party or member of the party's household, whether there is a continued risk of harm to the child or an abused party and which party can better provide adequate physical safeguards and supervision of the child.

(2.1) The information set forth in section 5329.1(a) (relating to consideration of child abuse and involvement with protective services).

(3) The parental duties performed by each party on behalf of the child.

(4)   The need for stability and continuity in the child's education, family life and community life.

(5)   The availability of extended family.

(6)   The child's sibling relationships.

(7)   The well-reasoned preference of the child, based on the child's maturity and judgment.

(8)   The attempts of a parent to turn the child against the other parent, except in cases of domestic violence where reasonable safety measures are necessary to protect the child from harm.

(9)   Which party is more likely to maintain a loving, stable, consistent and nurturing relationship with the child adequate for the child's emotional needs.

(10)   Which party is more likely to attend to the daily physical, emotional, developmental, educational and special needs of the child.

(11)   The proximity of the residences of the parties.

(12) Each party's availability to care
for the child or ability to make appropriate
child-care arrangements.

(13) The level of conflict between the
parties and the willingness and ability of the
parties to cooperate with one another. A
party's effort to protect a child from abuse
by another party is not evidence of
unwillingness or inability to cooperate with
that party.

(14) The history of drug or alcohol abuse
of a party or member of a party's household.

(15) The mental and physical condition of
a party or member of a party's household.

(16) Any other relevant factor.

Under 23 Pa.C.S.A. §5328, at the
conclusion of the custody trial, the court
must discuss the reasons for its decision in
open court or as part of the Order.

At some point, either by agreement or by court decision, a custody schedule will be in place. Once the schedule is made, if one parent needs a small change, try to be flexible when the request is reasonable and possible. This cooperation and flexibility with each other save trips to court and money. Make sure the adults handle the communications and decisions. Don't use the children as messengers.

Equitable Distribution Of Marital Property And Debt

In Pennsylvania, if requested, as part of the divorce, the courts will equitably divide the marital assets and/or debts. Equitable Distribution does not mean equal distribution.

According to Section 3501 of The Divorce Code, "marital property" means all property acquired by either party during the marriage and the increase in value of any non-marital property acquired pursuant to paragraphs (1) and (3) as measured and determined under subsection (a.1). However, marital property does not include:

(1) Property acquired prior to marriage or property acquired in exchange for property acquired prior to the marriage.

(2) Property excluded by valid agreement of the parties entered into before, during or after the marriage.

(3) Property acquired by gift, except between spouses, bequest, devise or descent or property acquired in exchange for such property.

(4) Property acquired after final separation until the date of divorce, except for property acquired in exchange for marital assets.

(5) Property which a party has sold, granted, conveyed or otherwise disposed of in good faith and for value prior to the date of final separation.

(6) Veterans' benefits exempt from attachment, levy or seizure pursuant to the act of September 2, 1958 (Public Law 85-857, 72 Stat. 1229), as amended, except for those benefits received by a veteran where the veteran has waived a portion of his military retirement pay in order to receive veterans' compensation.

(7) Property to the extent to which the property has been mortgaged or otherwise encumbered in good faith for value prior to the date of final separation.

(8) Any payment received as a result of an award or settlement for any cause of action or claim which accrued prior to the marriage or after the date of final separation regardless of when the payment was received.

(a.1) Measuring and determining the increase in value of nonmarital property.--The increase in value of any nonmarital property acquired pursuant to subsection (a)(1) and (3) shall be measured from the date of marriage or later acquisition date to either the date of final separation or the date as close to the hearing on equitable distribution as possible, whichever date results in a lesser increase. Any decrease in value of the nonmarital property of a party shall be offset against any increase in value of the nonmarital property of that party. However, a decrease in value of the nonmarital property of a party shall not be offset against any increase in value of the nonmarital property of the other party or against any other marital property subject to equitable division.

(b)   Presumption.--All real or personal property acquired by either party during the marriage is presumed to be marital property regardless of whether title is held individually or by the parties in some form of co-ownership such as joint tenancy, tenancy in common or tenancy by the entirety. The presumption of marital property is overcome by a showing that the property was acquired by a method listed in subsection (a). (c)   Defined benefit retirement plans.--Notwithstanding subsections (a), (a.1) and (b): (1)   In the case of the marital portion of a defined benefit retirement plan being distributed by means of a deferred distribution, the defined benefit plan shall be allocated between its marital and nonmarital portions solely by use of a coverture fraction. The denominator of the coverture fraction shall be the number of months the employee spouse worked to earn the total benefit and the numerator shall be the number of such months during which the parties were married and not finally separated.

The benefit to which the coverture fraction is applied shall include all postseparation enhancements except for enhancements arising from postseparation monetary contributions made by the employee spouse, including the gain or loss on such contributions.

(2) In the case of the marital portion of a defined benefit retirement plan being distributed by means of an immediate offset, the defined benefit plan shall be allocated between its marital and nonmarital portions solely by use of a coverture fraction. The denominator of the coverture fraction shall be the number of months the employee spouse worked to earn the accrued benefit as of a date as close to the time of trial as reasonably possible and the numerator shall be the number of such months during which the parties were married and not finally separated. The benefit to which the coverture fraction is applied shall include all postseparation enhancements up to a date as close to the time of trial as reasonably possible except for enhancements

arising from postseparation monetary
contributions made by the employee spouse,
including the gain or loss on such
contributions.

What triggers equitable distribution?
Section 3502 covers equitable division of
marital property.

> a) General rule-- Upon the request
> of either party in an action for
> divorce or annulment, the court
> shall equitably divide, distribute
> or assign, in kind or otherwise,
> the marital property between the
> parties without regard to marital
> misconduct in such percentages and
> in such manner as the court deems
> just after considering all relevant
> factors. The court may consider
> each marital asset or group of
> assets independently and apply a
> different percentage to each
> marital asset or group of assets.

Factors which are relevant to the
equitable division of marital property include
the following:

   (1)   The length of the marriage.

   (2)   Any prior marriage of either
party.

   (3)   The age, health, station, amount
and sources of income, vocational skills,
employability, estate, liabilities and
needs of each of the parties.

   (4)   The contribution by one party to
the education, training or increased
earning power of the other party.

   (5)   The opportunity of each party for
future acquisitions of capital assets and
income.

   (6)   The sources of income of both
parties, including, but not limited to,
medical, retirement, insurance or other
benefits.

   (7)   The contribution or dissipation
of each party in the acquisition,
preservation, depreciation or appreciation
of the marital property, including the
contribution of a party as homemaker.

(8) The value of the property set apart to each party.

(9) The standard of living of the parties established during the marriage.

(10) The economic circumstances of each party at the time the division of property is to become effective.

(10.1) The Federal, State and local tax ramifications associated with each asset to be divided, distributed or assigned, which ramifications need not be immediate and certain.

(10.2) The expense of sale, transfer or liquidation associated with a particular asset, which expense need not be immediate and certain.

(11) Whether the party will be serving as the custodian of any dependent minor children.

(b) Lien.--The court may impose a lien or charge upon property of a party as security for the payment of alimony or any other award for the other party.

(c) Family home.--The court may award, during the pendency of the action or otherwise, to one or both of the parties the right to reside in the marital residence.

(d) Life insurance.--The court may direct the continued maintenance and beneficiary designations of existing policies insuring the life or health of either party which were originally purchased during the marriage and owned by or within the effective control of either party. Where it is necessary to protect the interests of a party, the court may also direct the purchase of, and beneficiary designations on, a policy insuring the life or health of either party.

(e) Powers of the court.--If, at any time, a party has failed to comply with an order of equitable distribution, as provided for in this chapter or with the terms of an agreement as entered into between the parties, after hearing, the court may, in addition to any other remedy available under this part, in order to effect compliance with its order:

(1) enter judgment;

(2) authorize the taking and seizure of the goods and chattels and collection of the rents and profits of the real and personal, tangible and intangible property of the party;

(3)   award interest on unpaid installments;

(4)   order and direct the transfer or sale of any property required in order to comply with the court's order;

(5)   require security to insure future payments in compliance with the court's order;

(6)   issue attachment proceedings, directed to the sheriff or other proper officer of the county, directing that the person named as having failed to comply with the court order be brought before the court, at such time as the court may direct. If the court finds, after hearing, that the person willfully failed to comply with the court order, it may deem the person in civil contempt of court and, in its discretion, make an appropriate order, including, but not limited to, commitment of the person to the county jail for a period not to exceed six months;

(7)   award counsel fees and costs;

(8)   attach wages; or

(9)   find the party in contempt.

(f)   Partial distribution.--The
court, upon the request of either party,
may at any stage of the proceedings enter
an order providing for an interim partial
distribution or assignment of marital
property.

Section 3505 covers relief if there is
a disposition of property to defeat
obligations.

(a)   Preliminary relief.--Where it
appears to the court that a party is about
to leave the jurisdiction of the court or
is about to remove property of that party
from the jurisdiction of the court or is
about to dispose of, alienate or encumber
property in order to defeat equitable
distribution, alimony pendente lite,
alimony, child and spousal support or a
similar award, an injunction may issue to
prevent the removal or disposition and the
property may be attached as prescribed by
general rules. The court may also issue a
writ of ne exeat to preclude the removal.

(c) Discovery.--Discovery under this part shall be as provided for all other civil actions under the Pennsylvania Rules of Civil Procedure.

(d) Constructive trust for undisclosed assets.--If a party fails to disclose information required by general rule of the Supreme Court and in consequence thereof an asset or assets with a fair market value of $1,000 or more is omitted from the final distribution of property, the party aggrieved by the nondisclosure may at any time petition the court granting the award to declare the creation of a constructive trust as to all undisclosed assets for the benefit of the parties and their minor or dependent children, if any. The party in whose name the assets are held shall be declared the constructive trustee unless the court designates a different trustee, and the trust may include any terms and conditions the court may determine. The court shall grant the petition upon a finding of a failure to disclose the assets as required by general rule of the Supreme Court.

(e) Encumbrance or disposition to third parties.--An encumbrance or disposition of marital property to third persons who paid wholly inadequate consideration for the property may be deemed fraudulent and declared void.

As covered by section 3506, there is a Statement of reasons for distribution. In an order made under this chapter for the distribution of property, the court shall set forth the percentage of distribution for each marital asset or group of assets and the reason for the distribution ordered.

How Are Retirement Plans Treated In A Divorce?

Retirement plans are marital property if they are acquired during the marriage. For a retirement plan that existed prior to the marriage, the value range would be based from the date of marriage until the date of separation.

Retirement plans such as a 401(k) are pretty easy to determine the value of with the account statements. Pensions are more difficult to value and you and your attorney may need to hire an actuary to value the plan.

What Happens About Our
Health Insurance?

131

Very often both spouses are covered by the same health insurance plan through an employer. Once the parties divorce, one of them would no longer be eligible for coverage. A federal law called COBRA has sections addressing situations for spouses who lose their health benefits as a result of a divorce. The premium is usually at the employer's group rate so it may be cheaper than what can be found in the market. Payment of health insurance benefits can be addressed through the court or as part of a Marital Settlement Agreement.

What Is Alimony Pendente Lite?

Alimony pendente lite is an order for temporary support granted to a spouse during the pendency of a divorce or annulment proceeding.

Pennsylvania Rule of Civil Procedure 1910.4 outlines the calculation to be used in calculating an award. If the case involves children, the Alimony pendente lite award will be based on a 30% difference of the parties' net income. The award will account for the amount of child support obligation when coming up with the award amount. If the case does not involve children, then the amount of Alimony pendente lite is 40 percent of the non-dependent partie's net income.

Alimony

Alimony is an order for support granted by this Commonwealth or any other state to a spouse or former spouse in conjunction with a decree granting a divorce or annulment. Alimony starts after the court has granted the divorce. The court may award it as it deems reasonable only if it finds that alimony is necessary. When a party requests alimony, they will need to complete and submit a written monthly budget.

The Pennsylvania Divorce Code lists factors to be considered in awarding alimony.

They are:

(b) Factors relevant.--In determining whether alimony is necessary and in determining the nature, amount, duration and manner of payment of alimony, the court shall consider all relevant factors, including:

(1) The relative earnings and earning capacities of the parties.

(2) The ages and the physical, mental and emotional conditions of the parties.

(3) The sources of income of both parties, including, but not limited to, medical, retirement, insurance or other benefits.

(4)   The expectancies and inheritances of the parties.

(5)   The duration of the marriage.

(6)   The contribution by one party to the education, training or increased earning power of the other party.

(7)   The extent to which the earning power, expenses or financial obligations of a party will be affected by reason of serving as the custodian of a minor child.

(8)   The standard of living of the parties established during the marriage.

(9)   The relative education of the parties and the time necessary to acquire sufficient education or training to enable the party seeking alimony to find appropriate employment.

(10)   The relative assets and liabilities of the parties.

(11)   The property brought to the marriage by either party.

(12)   The contribution of a spouse as homemaker.

(13)   The relative needs of the parties.

(14)   The marital misconduct of either of the parties during the marriage. The marital misconduct of either of the parties from the date of final separation shall not be considered by the court in its determinations relative to alimony, except that the court shall consider the abuse of one party by the other party. As used in this paragraph, "abuse" shall have the meaning given to it under section 6102 (relating to definitions).

(15)   The Federal, State and local tax ramifications of the alimony award.

(16) Whether the party seeking alimony lacks sufficient property, including, but not limited to, property distributed under Chapter 35 (relating to property rights), to provide for the party's reasonable needs.

(17) Whether the party seeking alimony is incapable of self-support through appropriate employment.

(c) Duration.--The court in ordering alimony shall determine the duration of the order, which may be for a definite or an indefinite period of time which is reasonable under the circumstances.

(d) Statement of reasons.--In an order made under this section, the court shall set forth the reason for its denial or award of alimony and the amount thereof.

(e) Modification and termination.--An order entered pursuant to this section is subject to further order of the court upon changed circumstances of either party of a substantial and continuing nature whereupon the order may be modified, suspended, terminated or reinstituted or a new order made. Any further order shall apply only to payments accruing subsequent to the petition for the requested relief. Remarriage of the party receiving alimony shall terminate the award of alimony.

(f)   Status of agreement to pay alimony.-
-Whenever the court approves an agreement for
the payment of alimony voluntarily entered
into between the parties, the agreement shall
constitute the order of the court and may be
enforced as provided in section 3703 (relating
to enforcement of arrearages).

How Does Child Support Work?

Filing for Child Support

Most counties In Pennsylvania have walk in services to apply for support. There is an on-line intake questionnaire on the child support website. It can be found at: www.childsupport.state.pa.us. If you complete the online form and bring it with you, it could save you time later. If you choose, your attorney can also file for you. Pennsylvania has specific support guidelines within Pa R.C.P. 1910.16. The guidelines are based on the earnings of both parties. There will be situations where the court will assign an earning capacity.

An example of this is where someone intentionally quits a higher paying job for a lower paying job. The court will base their income at the higher amount.

When it comes to child support, your attorney will gather documents from you. With these documents your attorney will run tentative numbers for you to estimate the support amount.

These documents will include: past tax returns, documentation of any daycare costs, and costs of extracurricular activities the children participate in. You will need to document the cost of health insurance as well as dental and vision insurance. If you are collecting unemployment compensation, provide your attorney proof of that income. The same goes for any Social Security award letter if that applies to your situation. If there is a disability, you will need a letter verifying your physical condition. Provide information about any other support orders. You will need your W-2 as well as proof of payment for first and second mortgages.

After the filing is completed a support conference will be scheduled. You will need to complete and bring with you, the income and expense statement that you will receive in the mail. You and your attorney should have all of the documents (outlined above) available for the conference as well.

Also keep in mind that support amount adjustments can be made for substantial overnight stays (40-50%).

Based on the financial information and expenses provided, the officer will run a guideline support amount. That amount can be agreed to or you could end up agreeing to a deviated amount. There are also certain factors the trier of fact can consider to deviate from the standard support guidelines. These include: unusual needs and unusual fixed obligations, other support obligations of the parties, other income of the household, ages of the children, the relative assets and liabilities of the parties, medical expenses not covered by insurance, standard of living of the parties and their children. For spousal support or alimony pendente lite the duration of the marriage is considered and the court will consider other factors including the best interests of the child or children.

If the parties are unable to agree on the support, the case will then go in front of a hearing officer to determine the amount of support. This is an evidentiary hearing presided over by a hearing officer. Testimony will be given by both sides and there is an opportunity for questioning. At the conclusion, the hearing officer will adjourn it. They usually announce that he/she will notify the parties by mail of the support decision. The decision from the support hearing can be appealed.

Support orders can also be proposed by consent and submitted to the judge for his/her review and signature.

Support payments are usually collected through an employment wage attachment. The child support payments are collected and distributed by the State Collection and Disbursement Unit (SCDU). Depending on how your local system is set up, you will most likely be issued a credit card that the child support goes on or you may elect to sign up for direct deposit.

When a parent is not paying the required support, there are ways to enforce the Order.

Spousal Support

There are differences between spousal support and Alimony pendente lite. A case for spousal support can be filed whether or not anyone has filed for divorce. Spousal support ends when the divorce decree is granted. Alimony pendente lite can continue under certain factors.

The spouse causing the separation may not be entitled to spousal support. With alimony pendente lite, marital misconduct is usually irrelevant but there is an obligation to keep the divorce moving along.

Support orders can be modified if there has been a "material and substantial" change in circumstances. According to Pennsylvania Rules of Civil Procedure 1910.19(a), this request for modification is commenced by filing a petition with the court.

Legal Fees, Costs & Expenses

Within Section 3104 of the Pennsylvania Divorce Code, the court can order one party to pay for part or all of the other partie's legal fees, costs and expenses. This is most likely to occur only when there is a great difference in the economic resources of the parties.

Marital Settlement Agreement

Through the negotiations process, you can create a detailed Marital Settlement Agreement. This agreement can cover: division of the assets and debts, alimony/support, custody, child support, counsel fees/expenses, and tax issues. When you both agree, your attorney will prepare the settlement agreement. You both will initial each page and sign the final page.

If you have been unable to agree, these items will be decided over the course of the litigation through: Hearing Officers, Master's Hearings, and by the Judge's decisions.

Your Day In Court

"You armed me with strength for battle; you humbled my adversaries before me." Psalm 18:39

In Pennsylvania, a judge will decide many of the Family Law issues. The judge will listen to the testimony. Since they are the trier of fact, they will take notes. They also monitor the functioning of the trial and they make rulings on objections as they are raised by the attorneys. It is important to make a good impression with the judge. Here are some tips:

Don't be overly dramatic with waiving and flailing your arms, avoid making loud sighing sounds and outbursts and don't roll your eyes.

You want to appear calm and in control of your emotions. Remain calm and in control of yourself when others are speaking no matter how much you don't like what they are saying. You can make notes for your counsel and pass them to him/her so that they can read them and take any necessary actions.

Basics For Trial

Dress in a conservative business-casual manner. Don't wear anything flashy. Don't overdo the jewelry.

The amount of time scheduled for the trial will depend on the number of witnesses testifying and the number of issues involved. Some cases can be completed in part of a day and others can take several days.

The Process

The plaintiff (the person who initiated the action) will go first. He will be sworn in and enter the witness box. The attorney will complete their direct examination. Direct is the questions the attorney prepared to ask their client to draw out the testimony that supports their case.

After that is complete, the opposing attorney will ask their questions. This is called the cross-examination. These are questions to bring out the partie's weaknesses or to explore contradictions of fact.

If there are questions that are improper in the way they are asked or the subject matter the other attorney can make an objection.

It is important that when you are on the stand and the opposing attorney is asking you questions, when you are asked a question, do not immediately answer. Pause, then answer, this will give your attorney time to make any objections they need to make. If an objection is made, stop and wait until the judge makes a ruling on the objection to see if you are to answer the question or not.

After the cross examination there is re-direct. This is generally where the plaintiff's attorney asks questions as a follow up to cover anything that needs clarified from the cross examination. As an example, maybe you were asked something on cross examination that on the surface sounded damaging but you have a good explanation. This will be your chance to explain your prior answer.

If the opposing attorney wants to ask further questions based on those answers, they can re-cross. After all questions are answered the testimony is over. The next witness is called and the entire process occurs again. After the plaintiff's witnesses are all heard, the plaintiff rests and then it shifts to the other side to present their case in the same manner.

The judge may ask either side a few questions at the end of their testimony. At the conclusion of all testimony for both sides, depending on the type and complexity of the case, the judge may make a decision that will be delivered in writing at a later date. For other types of cases the judge may make an immediate oral decision right from the bench.

Isaiah 41:10 "So do not fear, for I am with you; do not be dismayed, for I am your God. I will strengthen you and help you; I will uphold you with my righteous right hand."

Relocations

Relocations are covered by section 5337 of the Divorce Code.

Relocations are to be done only after consent of the parties or by court approval. Parties proposing to relocate must provide notice sixty days prior to the proposed relocation. If the individual could not reasonably have known about the relocation in order to comply with the 60-day notice then notice must be given by the tenth day after the date the party knows of the relocation. The party must supply detailed information about the move. A counter-affidavit can be used to object to the proposed relocation. They are also required to give a warning that if non-relocating party does not object within 30 days after receipt of the notice, that party shall be foreclosed from objecting to the relocation.

If there is a filed objection on the counter-affidavit, a hearing shall be held as provided in subsection (g)(1). If no objection to the proposed relocation is filed under subsection (d), the party proposing the relocation shall file the following with the court prior to the relocation:

(1)   an affidavit stating that the party provided notice to every individual entitled to notice, the time to file an objection to the proposed relocation has passed and no individual entitled to receive notice has filed an objection to the proposed relocation;

(2)   Proof that proper notice was given in the form of a return receipt with the signature of the addressee and the full notice that was sent to the addressee.

(3)   a petition to confirm the relocation and modify any existing custody order; and

(4)   a proposed order containing the information set forth in subsection (c)(3).

(f) Modification of custody order.--If a
counter-affidavit regarding relocation is
filed with the court which indicates the
nonrelocating party both has no objection to
the proposed relocation and no objection to
the modification of the custody order
consistent with the proposal for revised
custody schedule, the court may modify the
existing custody order by approving the
proposal for revised custody schedule
submitted under subsection (c)(3)(viii), and
shall specify the method by which its future
modification can be made if desired by either
party. If a counter-affidavit regarding
relocation is filed with the court which
indicates the nonrelocating party objects
either to the proposed relocation or to the
modification of the custody order consistent
with the proposal for revised custody
schedule, the court shall modify the existing
custody order only after holding a hearing to
establish the terms and conditions of the
order pursuant to the relocation indicating
the rights, if any, of the nonrelocating
parties.

(g) Hearing.--

(1) Except as set forth in paragraph (3), the court shall hold an expedited full hearing on the proposed relocation after a timely objection has been filed and before the relocation occurs.

(2) Except as set forth in paragraph (3), the court may, on its own motion, hold an expedited full hearing on the proposed relocation before the relocation occurs.

(3) Notwithstanding paragraphs (1) and (2), if the court finds that exigent circumstances exist, the court may approve the relocation pending an expedited full hearing.

(4) If the court approves the proposed relocation, it shall:

(i) modify any existing custody order; or

(ii) establish the terms and conditions of a custody order.

(h)   Relocation factors.--In determining whether to grant a proposed relocation, the court shall consider the following factors, giving weighted consideration to those factors which affect the safety of the child:

(1)   The nature, quality, extent of involvement and duration of the child's relationship with the party proposing to relocate and with the nonrelocating party, siblings and other significant persons in the child's life.

(2)   The age, developmental stage, needs of the child and the likely impact the relocation will have on the child's physical, educational and emotional development, taking into consideration any special needs of the child.

(3)   The feasibility of preserving the relationship between the nonrelocating party and the child through suitable custody arrangements, considering the logistics and financial circumstances of the parties.

(4)   The child's preference, taking into consideration the age and maturity of the child.

(5)   Whether there is an established pattern of conduct of either party to promote or thwart the relationship of the child and the other party.

(6)   Whether the relocation will enhance the general quality of life for the party seeking the relocation, including, but not limited to, financial or emotional benefit or educational opportunity.

(7)   Whether the relocation will enhance the general quality of life for the child, including, but not limited to, financial or emotional benefit or educational opportunity.

(8)   The reasons and motivation of each party for seeking or opposing the relocation.

(9)   The present and past abuse committed by a party or member of the party's household and whether there is a continued risk of harm to the child or an abused party.

(10) Any other factor affecting the best interest of the child.

(i)   Burden of proof.--

(1) The party proposing the relocation has the burden of establishing that the relocation will serve the best interest of the child as shown under the factors set forth in subsection (h).

(2) Each party has the burden of establishing the integrity of that party's motives in either seeking the relocation or seeking to prevent the relocation.

(j) Failure to provide reasonable notice.--The court may consider a failure to provide reasonable notice of a proposed relocation as:

(1) a factor in making a determination regarding the relocation;

(2) a factor in determining whether custody rights should be modified;

(3) a basis for ordering the return of the child to the nonrelocating party if the relocation has occurred without reasonable notice;

(4) sufficient cause to order the party proposing the relocation to pay reasonable expenses and counsel fees incurred by the party objecting to the relocation; and

(5) a ground for contempt and the imposition of sanctions against the party proposing the relocation.

-(k) Mitigation.-Any consideration of a failure to provide reasonable notice under subsection (i) shall be subject to mitigation if the court determines that such failure was caused in whole, or in part, by abuse.

(l) Effect of relocation prior to hearing.--If a party relocates with the child prior to a full expedited hearing, the court shall not confer any presumption in favor of the relocation.

Final Thoughts

When you find yourself frustrated and overwhelmed remember to let emotions subside before you decide. Have confidence in yourself. You can get through this. Find something to be positive about each day. I wish you health, happiness and every success.

It is time to write the next chapter of your life!

CPSIA information can be obtained
at www.ICGtesting.com
Printed in the USA
LVOW04s1633140316

479091LV00018B/1085/P